Learn the ABCs
Kk
Warren Rylands and Samantha Nugent
LIGHTBOX
openlightbox.com

LIGHTBOX

Go to **www.openlightbox.com** and enter this book's unique code.

ACCESS CODE

LBXZ7979

Lightbox is an all-inclusive digital solution for the teaching and learning of curriculum topics in an original, groundbreaking way. Lightbox is based on National Curriculum Standards.

OPTIMIZED FOR

- ✓ TABLETS
- ✓ WHITEBOARDS
- ✓ COMPUTERS
- ✓ AND MUCH MORE!

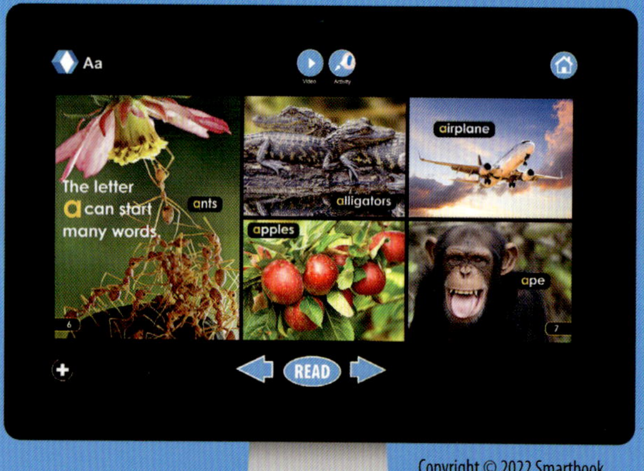

STANDARD FEATURES OF LIGHTBOX

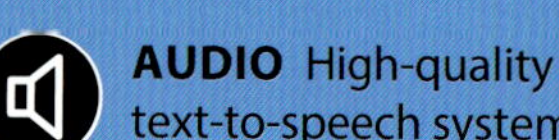

AUDIO High-quality narration using text-to-speech system

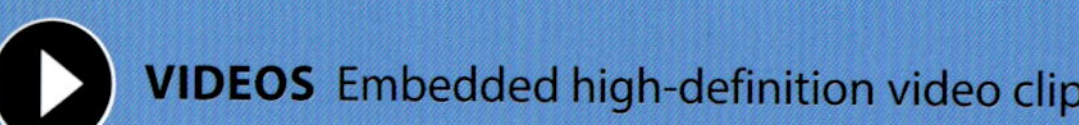

VIDEOS Embedded high-definition video clips

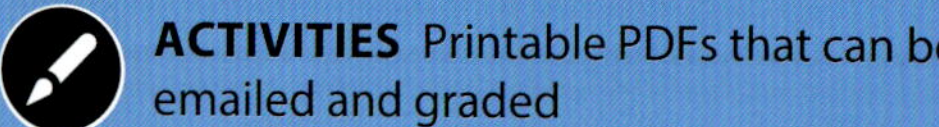

ACTIVITIES Printable PDFs that can be emailed and graded

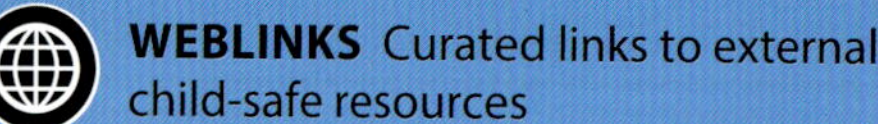

WEBLINKS Curated links to external, child-safe resources

SLIDESHOWS Pictorial overviews of key concepts

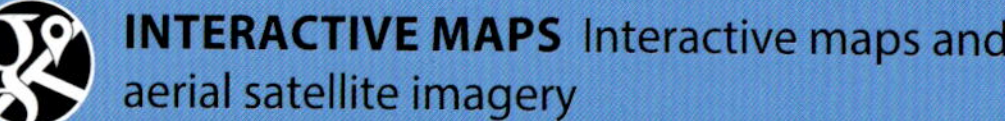

INTERACTIVE MAPS Interactive maps and aerial satellite imagery

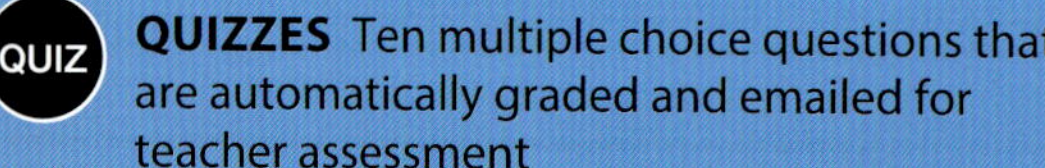

QUIZZES Ten multiple choice questions that are automatically graded and emailed for teacher assessment

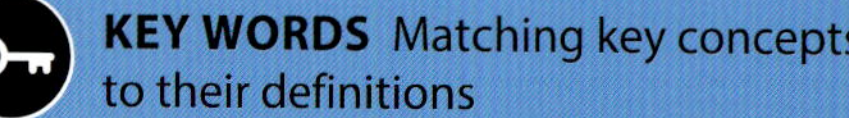

KEY WORDS Matching key concepts to their definitions

VIDEOS

WEBLINKS

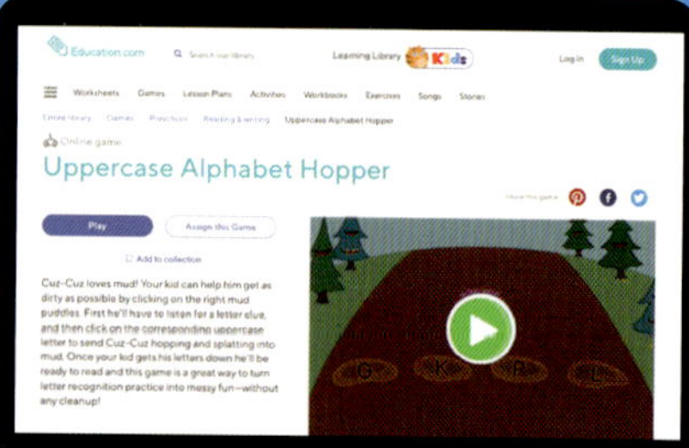

SLIDESHOWS

QUIZZES

This title is part of our Lightbox digital subscription

1-Year K–5 Subscription
ISBN 978-1-5105-5712-3

Access hundreds of Lightbox titles with our digital subscription. Sign up for a **FREE** subscription trial at **www.openlightbox.com/trial**

Kk

CONTENTS

2 Lightbox Access Code
4 Discovering the Letter K
6 Starting Words with K
8 K Inside a Word
10 Ending Words with K
12 Learning K Names
14 Different K Sounds
16 The K Sound
18 When K Stays Silent
20 Having Fun with K
22 K and the Alphabet
24 Key Words

Let's discover the letter

This is an uppercase K

This is how you write it

This is a lowercase k

This is how you write it

The letter **k** can start many words.

kangaroo

keys

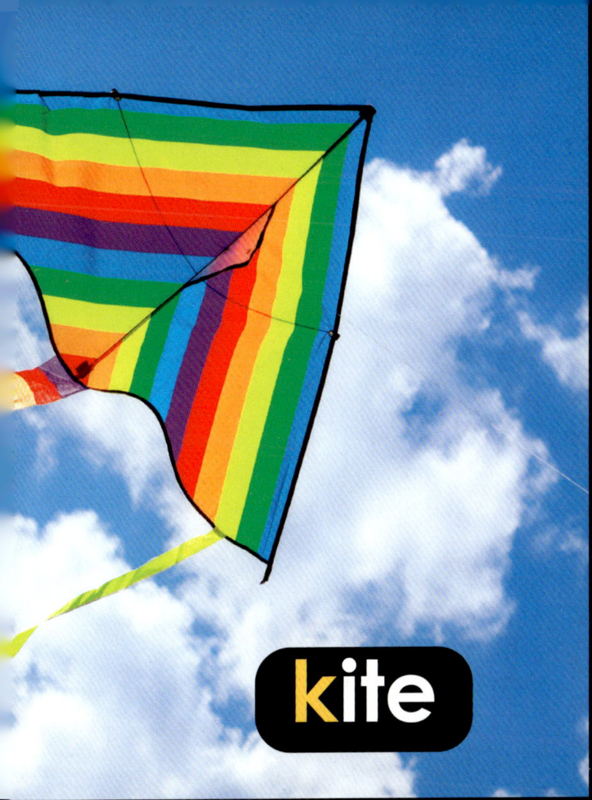

kite

kayak

Komodo dragon

The letter k can be inside a word.

gecko

skateboard
pickle

The letter k can be at the end of a word.
shark
rock

clock
pink
hawk

Many names start with an uppercase K.

Kelly bakes cookies.

Katie loves giraffes.

Keith is tall.

Kim likes to read.

Ken learns to ride a bike.

The letter **k** can make a sound or stay quiet.

kitten

knit

The letter k makes a sound in the word **kitten**.

The letter k does not make a sound in the word **knit**.

The letter k makes a sound in most words.

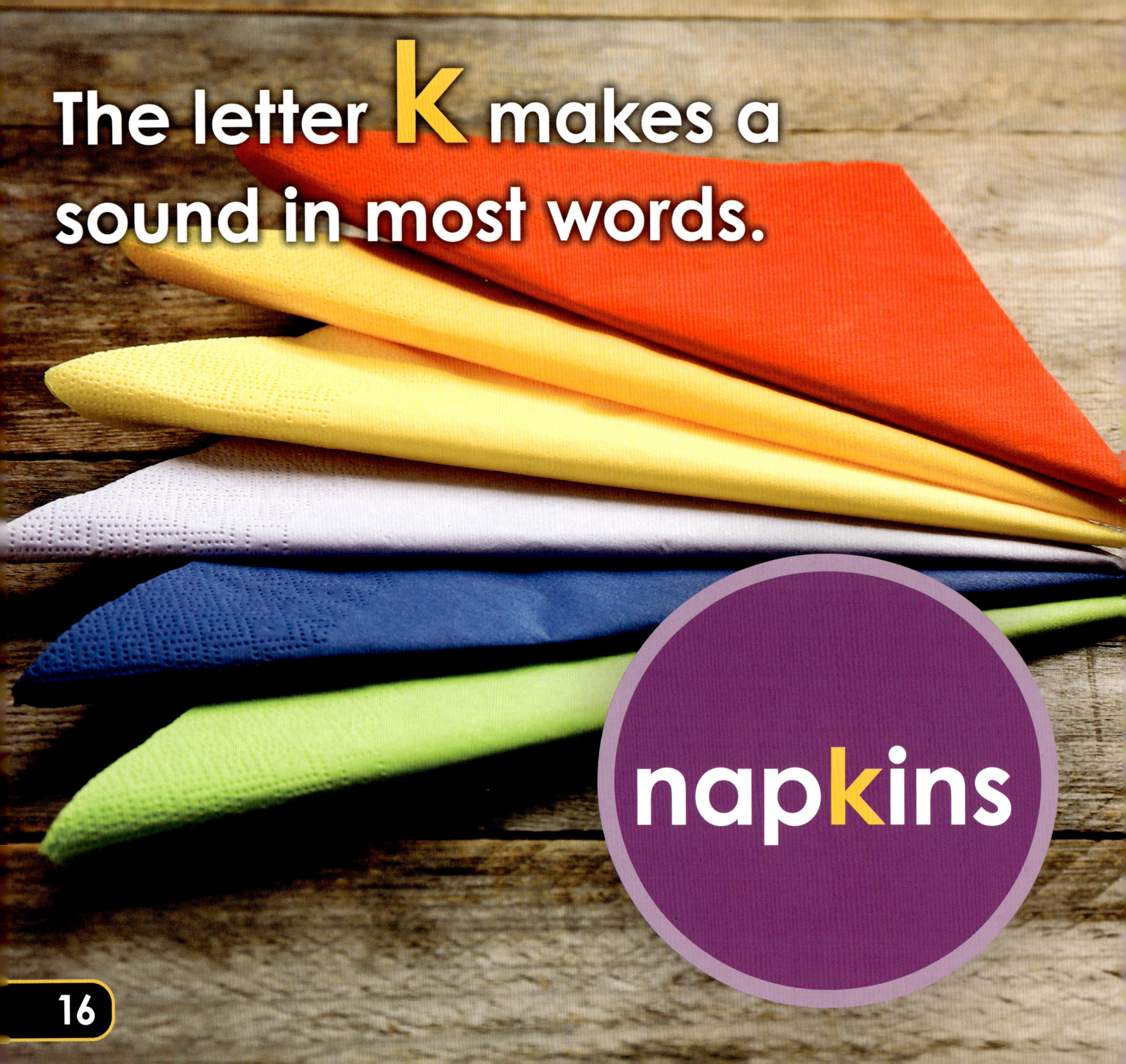

ask
keep
kiss
back

The letter k does not make a sound when it comes before the letter n.

knee

know

knot

knight

Having Fun with K

Kelly the kangaroo likes pickles.

Kevin the shark knows pickles keep Kelly happy.

Kevin asked the knight on the bike for pickles.

The knight had pickles in his back pocket.

Kevin took the pickles to Kelly's black shack.

That was kind of Kevin!

The alphabet has 26 letters.

K is the eleventh letter in the alphabet.

Aa Bb Cc Dd

Ee Ff Gg Hh Ii Jj

Kk Ll Mm Nn Oo

Pp Qq Rr Ss Tt Uu

Vv Ww Xx Yy Zz

KEY WORDS

Research has shown that as much as 65 percent of all written material published in English is made up of 300 words. These 300 words cannot be taught using pictures or learned by sounding them out. They must be recognized by sight. This book contains 48 common sight words to help young readers improve their reading fluency and comprehension. This book also teaches young readers several important content words, such as proper nouns. These words are paired with pictures to aid in learning and improve understanding.

Page	Sight Words First Appearance
4	let, letter, the
5	a, an, how, is, it, this, write, you
6	can, many, start, words
8	be
10	at, end, of
12	names, with
13	learn, likes, read, to
14	make, or, sound
15	does, in, not
16	most
17	ask, back, keep
18	before, comes, when
19	know
21	for, on
21	had, his, kind, that, took, was
22	has

Page	Content Words First Appearance
4	Kk
6	kangaroo, key
7	kayak, kite, Komodo dragon
8	bike, gecko, hike
9	pickle, skateboard
10	rock, shark
11	clock, hawk, pink
12	cookies, Kelly
13	giraffes, Katie, Keith, Ken, Kim
14	kitten
16	napkins
17	kiss
18	knee
19	knife, knight, knot
20	fun, Kevin
21	pocket, shack
22	alphabet

Published by Smartbook Media Inc.
276 5th Avenue, Suite 704 #917
New York, NY 10001
Website: www.openlightbox.com

Library of Congress Cataloging-in-Publication Data

Names: Rylands, Warren, author. | Nugent, Samantha, author.
Title: Kk / Warren Rylands and Samantha Nugent.
Description: New York : Smartbook Media Inc., [2022] | Series: Learn the ABCs | Audience: Grades K-1.
Identifiers: LCCN 2020054170 (print) | LCCN 2020054171 (ebook) | ISBN 9781510557659 (library binding) | ISBN 9781510557673 (ebook other)
Subjects: LCSH: English language--Consonants--Juvenile literature. | English language--Alphabet--Juvenile literature.
Classification: LCC PE1165 .R9532 2022 (print) | LCC PE1165 (ebook) | DDC 421/.1--dc23
LC record available at https://lccn.loc.gov/2020054170
LC ebook record available at https://lccn.loc.gov/2020054171

Printed in Guangzhou, China
1 2 3 4 5 6 7 8 9 0 25 24 23 22 21

022021
110820

Art Director: Terry Paulhus **Project Coordinator:** Sara Cucini

The publisher acknowledges Getty Images as the primary image supplier for this title.